The Heart and Soul Animal Sanctuary

To Love and Be Loved

For Doyle,
Thank you for loving animals,

Natalie Owings

2009

The Heart and Soul Animal Sanctuary

To Love and Be Loved

Natalie Owings

photographs by
Tracy Sweetman

SUNSTONE
PRESS
SANTA FE

Sunstone books may be purchased for educational, business, or sales promotional use.
For information please write: Special Markets Department, Sunstone Press, P.O. Box 2321, Santa Fe, New Mexico 87504-2321.

Body typeface ∞ Nueva Std 12
Printed on acid free paper

Library of Congress Cataloging-in-Publication Data

Owings, Natalie, 1939-
The Heart and Soul Animal Sanctuary : to love and be loved / by Natalie Owings ; with photographs by Tracy Sweetman.
p. cm.
ISBN 978-0-86534-708-3 (hardcover : alk. paper)
1. Heart and Soul Animal Sanctuary. 2. Animal rescue--New Mexico. I. Title.
HV4765.N6O85 2008
636.08'320978956--dc22
2008048507

Published in Santa Fe

WWW.SUNSTONEPRESS.COM
SUNSTONE PRESS / POST OFFICE BOX 2321 / SANTA FE, NM 87504-2321 /USA
(505) 988-4418 / ORDERS ONLY (800) 243-5644 / FAX (505) 988-1025

For information regarding the photographs contact Ms. Sweetman via e-mail: miss_october@mac.com

"My work is inspired by my life. I express myself through my photographs. Everything that surrounds me provokes my feelings."
—André Kertész

For the abused and abandoned animals
of the world, and those who save them.

Preface

The Heart and Soul Animal Sanctuary is a natural evolution of strong feelings and many experiences. Growing up on a ranch in New Mexico was influential. Our dog, Pooch, was a typical stray dog, about fifty pounds, tan, and extremely loveable. He wandered in one day and stayed. If only Pooch knew what a profound impression he made on my then very young mind. I still adore him and hope to be with him again one day.

I have never been able to walk past or drive past a lost and starving dog. Such destitution, such misery and such fright they must experience. It is always a relief to me to have rescued such a dog or puppy. It started in my home, but with no particular plans, no "sanctuary" in mind. But the sanctuary was inevitable. At this writing I rescued my first dog more than 30 years ago.

Reading the writings of Albert Schweitzer through the years has compounded my own determination and motivation to rescue as many abandoned animals as possible. His time was devoted to the impoverished and ill natives of equatorial Africa. My time is devoted to the impoverished and ill dogs and puppies of the American Southwest. Even though I work all day, every day, with two staff members to help clean and feed, our efforts result in so little, because there are so many in need. I am thankful that the animals we take in are blissfully happy but I wish we could do much, much more. It is only a matter of money. More money makes more sanctuaries possible.

Every dog, every puppy, every cat and kitten, every horse and foal, every duck, goose and chicken and rabbit and guinea pig is a masterpiece in itself. I believe that the human species has not come to realize how exquisitely beautiful and uniquely special animals are. We tend to disregard them as unimportant and without value. So many species have fallen into extinction at the ruthless, greedy hands of man. We must reconsider.

My hope is that things are changing. Many individuals

are attempting to start sanctuaries. I try to be of help to each one through practical advice. My hope is also to convey the value of adopting a rescued dog or puppy rather than buying one. When I watch an abused dog come into the sanctuary, frightened, starved, and with no feelings of trust, my heart goes out to this creature. We grant such a dog or puppy everything he needs, and more: wonderful food, medical care, friends all around, soft beds, fun, walks in the mountains every day, and of course hugs and more hugs. The dogs are transformed within a few days. I love to look into their happy eyes, to feel their sparse coats become fluffy, to watch their tails rise up and wag.

The Heart and Soul Animal Sanctuary is located in Glorieta, New Mexico on 130 acres of donated land. It is in the Sangre de Cristo Mountains at an elevation of 7500 to 8000 feet, 15 miles from Santa Fe. Pine forest covers these mountains making habitat for the animals peaceful and beautiful summer or winter. Visitors are welcome and arrive almost daily. The sanctuary cares for approximately 150 animals at all times: dogs, puppies, cats, kittens, horses, llamas, goats, rabbits, guinea pigs, ducks, geese and chickens. There are no cages. Everyone has a home. Chain link fence is not permitted. The sanctuary buildings are all constructed of rough sawn wood so as to blend with the forest setting. Dogs and puppies run free.

I am grateful that it has been possible to create a sanctuary like ours in such a needy place as New Mexico. The great numbers of abandoned and abused animals does not slow down, so we remain extremely busy at all times. Veterinary medicine is very demanding financially. Our newsletter helps to raise the necessary funds. This is a non-profit tax-exempt organization. All donations are tax deductible. Mailing address: The Heart and Soul Animal Sanctuary, 369 Montezuma Avenue, No. 130, Santa Fe, NM 87501. Phone: (505) 757-6817.

Blessings to all the animals of our world, and to those of you who love them.

—Natalie Owings, Director and Founder

Natalie Owings and Friends
Photograph by Norah Levine,
courtesy of the *Santa Fean Magazine*

All Creatures Large and Small

by
Ashleigh Morris
from
The Santa Fean

atalie Owings renews faith in humanity through her Heart and Soul Animal Sanctuary.

For New Mexico's animals in need, Natalie Owings is a godsend. Wherever she goes on Heart and Soul Animal Sanctuary reserve, which she formally founded as a nonprofit and tends round-the-clock, she's surrounded by an impressively well-behaved pack of mongrels: some tripods, others nursing stitches or new litters, all of them abused, neglected, or discarded yet somehow made whole again by this amazing animal whisperer. "We concentrate on making everyone superbly happy," says Owings, "because they've all had such dreadful beginnings." Be they abandoned canines or kitties, geese, llamas, horses, or even guinea pigs, she cares for them, often saving them from euthanasia at area shelters. "I've always done this,"

says Owings about helping every creature in sight since her childhood in Pojoaque. "My mother was beside herself with all the things I'd rescue." She likes to quote Albert Schweitzer and Ghandi when reminding us to be more compassionate, having witnessed humanity's darker side for decades. "I see an amazing misunderstanding of other species," she says, finding hope in the small miracle of saving these once-mistreated souls. "All I can do is try," she says, and thank goodness for us—and for them—she does.

The sanctuary, near the Pecos Wilderness, is open for tours by appointment; youth groups are encouraged in the summer. Financial donations are needed most (vet bills for her nearly 150 animals can cost $5,000 a month); a wish list is available online. Some dogs and cats can be adopted, though many will gratefully live out their lives in Owings's care.

The Heart and Soul Animal Sanctuary

To Love and Be Loved

If we open our hearts to
other creatures and allow
ourselves to sympathize with
their joys and struggles,
we find they have the strength
to touch and transform us.
There is an inwardness in other
creatures that awakens what
is innermost in ourselves.

— Gary Kowalski

The dogs enjoy resting on high rocks in the mountains. They sit and rest as individuals, yet they are together.
They find happy companionship as a group, yet they respect one another's barriers and space. I find integrity in their ways.
It is a fulfilling joy to respect other living beings for exactly who and what they are. Then we are more together as one.

SLOW DOWN AND ENJOY LIFE.
IT'S NOT ONLY THE SCENERY
YOU MISS BY GOING TOO FAST.
YOU ALSO MISS THE SENSE
OF WHERE YOU ARE GOING,
AND WHY.

→ EDDIE CANTOR

Lacey came to the sanctuary as a 10 month old emaciated and frightened youngster.
Her eyes are permanently weakened by early malnutrition. She required surgery on her smashed hip immediately.
She lost a litter of puppies and she was a puppy herself. And more. But Lacey is a child of the angels. She is love exemplified.

UNTIL ONE HAS LOVED
AN ANIMAL, A PART OF
ONE'S SOUL REMAINS
UNAWAKENED.

— ANATOLE FRANCE

(1844 - 1924)

This thoughtful puppy was rescued with her five litter mates in Tesuque, New Mexico. Their mother had died, and the puppies were abandoned. Many beautiful litters of abandoned puppies have come to the sanctuary. After feeling lost and frightened the puppies come to be happy and playful and to thrive. What sunshine is to flowers, playful puppies are to the heart.

DO NOT GO WHERE THE PATH
MAY LEAD ; GO INSTEAD WHERE
THERE IS NO PATH AND LEAVE
A TRAIL .

— RALPH WALDO EMERSON

(1803 · 1882)

This is one of the sanctuary's fascinating young hunt-by-sight dogs, Emmie; she has a passion in her heart for hunting down
any sort of treasure. Emmie and her sister, Fudgie, arrived from a reservation in sickly condition, and painfully shy.
In three months, with rehabilitation and affection, medical care and good food, Emmie and Fudgie became ravishing.
It was then that many people wished to adopt one of them. But it is their destiny to live here at the sanctuary, together, in perfect harmony.

THE OTHER NIGHT IN THE FREEZING RAIN,
THAT LITTLE FEMALE CAME AGAIN.
MATTED AND SOAKED, CRYING IN NEED,
LOST AND ALONE WITH BABIES TO FEED.
HER PLEADING EYES I COULDN'T IGNORE,
THERE'S ALWAYS ROOM FOR ONE MORE.

— AUTHOR UNKNOWN

To our dismay, there are always more abandoned mother dogs with puppies to feed. Pregnant dogs looking for shelter to bear their young are often found on the streets, the open road, or the countryside. Sometimes mother dogs give birth in shelters, sometimes in culverts. Why is a mother dog abandoned just when she needs help most? Too much trouble … more mouths to feed … Why wasn't the mother spayed? Too much trouble … too much cost … So the sanctuary takes in as many mother dogs as possible; it is indeed an honor. The puppies are always beautiful beings who adore life. It is a joy to watch them grow and become part of the world.

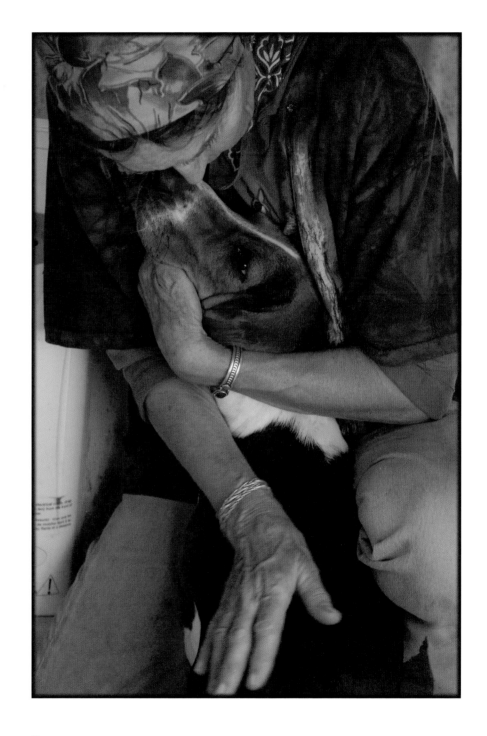

I HAVE ONLY TWO KINDS OF DAYS:
HAPPY AND HYSTERICALLY HAPPY.

— ALLEN J. LEFFERDINK

Daisy, our laughing, smiling dog, with one ear up and one down, came to the sanctuary at the tender age of ten days. She was one in a litter of five abandoned puppies with no mother. Daisy was not born into good fortune and prosperity; she was born in a poor town hidden from view and noticed only by her mother. But for Daisy every day is sheer sunshine and joy, a girl of positive felicity. She is possessed by bliss. If one is experiencing a disquieting day, it is time to take a walk with Daisy.

WHETHER ONE BELIEVES IN A
RELIGION OR NOT...
THERE ISN'T ANYONE WHO
DOESN'T APPRECIATE KINDNESS
AND COMPASSION.

— MAHATMA GANDHI

(1869 - 1948)

Little Ivy and her four litter mates came from desolation and deprivation of all kinds. The litter had been exposed to distemper.
One died. The others survived. It was a wretched experience and the pups were pitiful upon arrival at the sanctuary.
But the misfortunes and sufferings of an animal bid us to help. Compassion is what a lost animal aches for.
We can allay their distress simply by pouring out feelings of pity and love. Their bodies surrender in relaxation and peace.
Then they can learn to trust, to bond with their new human friends. Life is OK to live after all.

UNTIL WE EXTEND THE CIRCLE
OF OUR COMPASSION TO ALL LIVING
THINGS WE WILL NOT OURSELVES
FIND PEACE.

— ALBERT SCHWEITZER

(1875 - 1965)

On a winter day a litter of seven puppies was seen venturing out of their cave where they were born. Their feral mother stood nearby. This was her fourth litter to be born in this cave. Food was provided daily. At seven weeks of age the puppies were taken to the sanctuary. Otherwise their future would be uncertain. Hungry coyotes run through these hills.

WE APPRECIATE WHAT WE SHARE;
WE DO NOT APPRECIATE WHAT
WE RECEIVE.
FRIENDSHIP, AFFECTION IS NOT
ACQUIRED BY GIVING PRESENTS.
FRIENDSHIP, AFFECTION COMES ABOUT
BY TWO SHARING A SIGNIFICANT
MOMENT, BY HAVING AN EXPERIENCE
IN COMMON.

— ABRAHAM JOSHUA HESCHEL

(1907 – 1972)

Among my friends I count the dogs. Among the dogs I know that Spirit shares my heart.
No one will ever be able to measure the depth of heart between dog and man.
From these hearts together grows an indescribable spring of life.

GREATNESS LIES NOT IN BEING STRONG,
BUT IN THE RIGHT USE OF STRENGTH;
AND STRENGTH IS NOT USED RIGHTLY
WHEN IT ONLY SERVES TO CARRY A MAN
ABOVE HIS FELLOWS FOR HIS OWN
SOLITARY GLORY.
HE IS GREATEST WHOSE STRENGTH
CARRIES UP THE MOST HEARTS BY
THE ATTRACTION OF HIS OWN.

— HENRY WARD BEECHER

(1813 - 1887)

And so it is with the sanctuary top dog, Spirit, that when his decision is made, the others always follow along. He keeps pace with the tasks before him and every situation is important. He enables the little ones to feel protected. Spirit was found in a gas station as a starving puppy. He is a pathfinder among dogs and has lived as a gentle leader at the sanctuary.

FRIENDS — THEY CHERISH
EACH OTHER'S HOPES.
THEY ARE KIND TO EACH
OTHER'S DREAMS.

— HENRY DAVID THOREAU

(1817 – 1862)

Sharing among puppies is remarkably visible. Here, a three month old comes to share a moment with a three and a half week old puppy. The older pup understands that the little one is smaller and weaker. There is no competition, only understanding. Among puppies, the road to a friend's house is never long. Puppies growing up among older dogs learn all they need to know about barriers, boundaries and respect in a short time.

MOST DOGS DON'T THINK
THEY ARE HUMAN;
THEY KNOW THEY ARE.

— JANE SWANN

The little dog's name was Nana, but could have been "Devotion." Human companionship was Nana's paradise.
She arrived at the sanctuary rather lost and forlorn, with puppies to raise. But Nana found joy in being cared for by humans.
She mostly ignored the other dogs because, as the saying goes, she knew in her special heart she was a human.

IF A BLADE OF GRASS HAS
THE POWER TO MOVE YOU,
IF THE SIMPLE THINGS OF NATURE
HAVE A MESSAGE THAT YOU UNDERSTAND,
REJOICE FOR YOUR SOUL IS ALIVE.

— ELEANOR DUSE

(1858 - 1924)

Catching a sniff of a yellow wildflower, Regie seemed so appreciative of this piece of botanical nature. He stopped short during a fast race down the mountainside to pay this plant his respects. Regie is three and a half months old in this photo. He arrived at the sanctuary in a tiny litter of six newborns, two days old, with his exhausted, emaciated mother, Gracie. Gracie had been abandoned as a pregnant, weak mother in a New Mexico town. Gracie and the pups were brought to us where she collapsed in her warm, cozy nursery. After a few days, and learning to trust, she felt free to smile. She raised her six pups like a tidy, devoted Swiss nursemaid.

I FIND IT WHOLESOME TO BE ALONE
THE GREATER PART OF THE TIME...
I LOVE TO BE ALONE.
I NEVER FOUND THE COMPANION THAT
WAS SO COMPANIONABLE AS SOLITUDE.
WE ARE FOR THE MOST PART
MORE LONELY WHEN WE GO ABROAD
AMONG MEN THAN WHEN WE STAY
IN OUR CHAMBERS.
A MAN THINKING OR WORKING IS
ALWAYS ALONE; LET HIM BE
WHERE HE WILL.

— HENRY DAVID THOREAU

(1817 - 1862)

In the world of dogs we have so many fine characters. Our rescued mama basset hound, Auntie Mae, speaks to us of great gentility. She must have been well born with courage and self respect. Auntie Mae was found abandoned under a vehicle in Las Vegas, New Mexico, with seven newborn puppies. The sanctuary received her gratefully and helped Auntie Mae raise her beautiful pups. One, Peaches, remains here with Auntie Mae. She daily speaks of respect and love for all.

IF A DOG WILL NOT COME
TO YOU AFTER HAVING LOOKED
YOU IN THE FACE, YOU SHOULD
GO HOME AND EXAMINE
YOUR CONSCIENCE.

— WOODROW WILSON

(1856 - 1924)

Dogs and puppies are indeed capable of deciphering what sort of mood or state of mind their human is in. This beautiful white puppy, named Fudgie, was found abandoned and hungry on a reservation. She is especially perceptive and observant. An Irish wolfhound by heritage, she has formed a very strong bond with me, as they are known to do. Fudgie plays wildly with her sister, Emmie, requiring a great deal of time and space. Being sight hounds it is a joy to watch their power and speed while running together through the mountains. At night they rest silently and beautifully, a work of art.

OH, WHAT A GLORY THIS WORLD
PUTS ON, FOR HIM WHO WITH A
FERVENT HEART GOES FORTH UNDER
THE BRIGHT AND GLORIOUS SKY,
AND LOOKS ON DUTIES WELL
PERFORMED, AND DAYS WELL SPENT.

— HENRY WADSWORTH LONGFELLOW

(1807 - 1882)

This forever thoughtful and delicate countenance is Luke. Luke was born on a cold January day in a large city shelter. His tiny mother had given birth to three beautiful tan Dachsund-cross puppies. She was shivering cold and trying to keep her puppies warm amidst the chaos of cleaning the shelter, slamming doors and garbage cans. Fortunately my friend traveled to the shelter, picked up the little family of four, and drove them 75 miles to the sanctuary. The shivering mother dog, whom I named Dreamy, was terrified of people. However, Dreamy settled into her warm, quiet nursery and proceeded to raise her pups in peace. Dreamy was so afraid I could not even touch her for two weeks. Then one day everything was blissful for her. She was emerging from a world of abuse and terror and becoming a beam of sunshine, warm and loving. Dreamy and two of her beloved pups remain permanently and happily at the sanctuary.

THE PLEASANTEST THINGS IN THE
WORLD ARE PLEASANT THOUGHTS,
AND THE GREATEST ART IN LIFE
IS TO HAVE AS MANY OF THEM
AS POSSIBLE.

— JOHN FOSTER

(1836 - 1917)

A small, tan, scruffy little dog was standing in a box in my driveway some years ago. Someone had put her there.
Such a lovely smile and sparkling eyes this rather unkempt small creature had. I carried her
(and she was so willing) up the driveway and into the sanctuary house. I named the dear one Posie.
Posie immediately got along well with all the other dogs, large and small, and she continued to be everybody's best friend through the years.
She is a master of pleasant thought, and walks along every day as though all the world is one giant pleasantry. Thank heaven for little Posies.

REST IS NOT IDLENESS, AND
TO LIE SOMETIMES ON A SUMMER
DAY LISTENING TO THE MURMUR
OF WATER, OR WATCHING THE
CLOUDS FLOAT ACROSS THE SKY,
IS HARDLY A WASTE OF TIME.

→ SIR JOHN WILLIAM LUBBOCK

(1803 - 1865)

Puppies at the sanctuary, like puppies everywhere, are soft little angels while sound asleep. Nature has granted puppies the ability to sleep deeply even in the midst of noise. They will sleep soundly for long periods of time; indeed a puppy should not be awakened since sleep is such an important part of their growth and development. This beautiful puppy was rescued from abandonment, spent two and a half weeks at the sanctuary, and was adopted into a loving home.

AMONG TRUE AND REAL FRIENDS,
ALL IS COMMON;
AND WERE IGNORANCE AND ENVY
AND SUPERSTITION BANISHED FROM
THE WORLD, ALL MANKIND WOULD
BE FRIENDS.

—PERCY BYSSHE SHELLEY

(1792 - 1822)

Many dogs live together at the sanctuary, varying greatly in size and age. When dogs are well treated, fed well, and permitted plenty of exercise they become very good friends. They grant the sentiments of esteem, respect and affection to the top dog and find pleasure in his welfare. The dogs play together, chew biscuits together, run together, hunt together all the day long. When hungry and tired they eat together. They share beds and some sleep against and among one another. It is profoundly gratifying to observe the fairness and the interest they have in one another. Where a simple growl will do, there is no bite. If only mankind could learn how to live in peace, from a group of dogs.

DON'T TRY TO TELL ME
ANY HUMAN COULD
LOVE YOU MORE THAN
I DO!

— UNKNOWN

Lilly, a gorgeous border collie-heeler combination, a herding dog to the core, came to the sanctuary with seven newborn puppies. Lilly was only one year old. It became evident that Lilly was ill as she was not up to nursing her pups. A trip to the veterinary hospital revealed that Lilly had pyometra; her infected uterus had to be evacuated or she would perish. While Lilly was hospitalized we fed her babies well; ne'er a complaint. When Lilly returned she nurtured her puppies lovingly. There was no attempt on their part to nurse. Sometimes, among dogs, nature knows best. Lilly continues to this day to be a sanctuary country dog, herding everyone else along. She is a treasure.

No one appreciates the
very special genius of
your conversations as
a dog does.

— Christopher Morley

(1890 – 1957)

While sitting on a large rock with several dogs and watching the sun lowering through the trees, little blonde Emma came prancing to have a conversation and a kiss. Emma is delicate and sweet but very playful too. It is horrifying to realize she was taken to a scary dog pound for euthanasia. Emma was rescued from the euthanasia list and delivered to the sanctuary. For the first week she hid behind pillows and under shelves. But Emma was too loved by her new dog and human friends to have this hiding last long. The lovely little Tibetan spaniel sprang into sanctuary life, glowing, playing, and loving everyone. She is a special treasure, living permanently with all of us at the sanctuary.

A DOG HAS THE SOUL

OF A PHILOSOPHER.

— PLATO

(427 - 347 B.C.)

Found running astray on ranch land, this fascinating small dog was starving. How he got there, no one knows. Perry was chasing baby goats out of hunger. Fortunately, a compassionate person witnessed the chase. She saved the baby goats and Perry too. Perry came to the sanctuary and made it his home immediately. Though some people wished to adopt him it would not work out. Perry is a sanctuary dog, a hunter, a friend, a thoroughly pleasant character, and a dignified philosopher.

THE ART OF LIVING IS
ALWAYS TO MAKE A GOOD
THING OUT OF A BAD
THING.

E. F. SCHUMACHER

(1911 - 1977)

Sometimes puppies arrive at the sanctuary who are not well and who need to be hospitalized. Little Moosie was such a puppy. He was rescued from a desolate area of the Southwest and brought to the sanctuary along with his sibling brother. Their rescue was not a moment too soon. Both puppies were very malnourished and they suffered from intestinal bacterial infections and parasites. Moosie was the quiet observant one who never complained. He seemed to understand that now someone cared and he was being helped. Moosie came through his puppy illness and is growing up at the sanctuary to be a large and loving German shepherd cross. What Moosie loves is to be hugged, an indescribable pleasure.

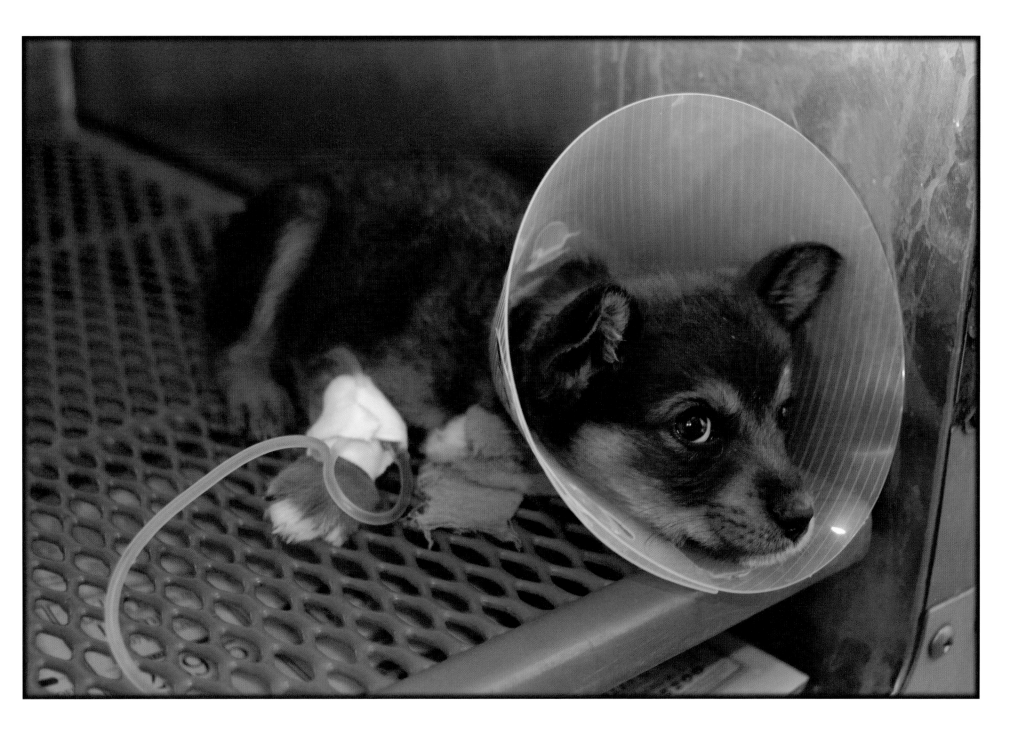

I SHALL PASS THROUGH THIS WORLD
BUT ONCE .
ANY GOOD THEREFORE THAT I CAN
DO , OR ANY KINDNESS THAT I
CAN SHOW TO ANY BEING , LET ME
DO IT NOW.
LET ME NOT DEFER OR NEGLECT
IT, FOR I SHALL NOT PASS
THIS WAY AGAIN .

— HENRY DRUMMOND

(1851 - 1897)

Puppies love to sleep in heaps together for warmth and security. These three and a half week old pups were found sick and abandoned.
One had a broken tibia. The splint was wrapped in bandages to keep the puppy's leg straight and had to be changed periodically.
But the puppy was always playful and happy and loved his four siblings.
Puppies grant meaning to each others' lives through their love and dependence on each other.

NO LANGUAGE CAN EXPRESS THE
POWER AND BEAUTY AND HEROISM
OF A MOTHER'S LOVE.
IT SHRINKS NOT WHERE MAN COWERS,
AND GROWS STRONGER WHERE MAN
FAINTS, AND OVER THE WASTES
OF WORLDLY FORTUNE SENDS THE
RADIANCE OF ITS QUENCHLESS FIDELITY
LIKE A STAR IN HEAVEN.

— EDWIN HUBBELL CHAPIN

(1814 - 1880)

Beautiful Hannah arrived at the sanctuary with six newborn puppies. Hannah was an abandoned mother dog found in the southern part of the state of New Mexico. She seemed to trust right away that she and her newborns had arrived in the right place. Hannah was a superb and devoted mother spending long days and nights in attendance to her puppies, washing, nursing and nurturing as only a mother dog can. Hannah came to adore sanctuary life, manifesting her great desire for social life. She befriended every other dog and established a convivial relationship with each one, although she seemed to find some more socially acceptable than others. All the puppies look exactly like their mama except that they are all black. Who is papa? Only beautiful Hannah knows …

LIVING JEWELS,

DROPPED UNSTAINED,

FROM HEAVEN.

— ROBERT POLLOCK

(1798 - 1827)

Such warm, soft bundles of contentment are the newborn puppies. Their mothers are in close attendance to oversee the welfare of each one, to make sure each one is fed and washed. It is a wonder of nature how beautiful and complete each puppy is, and consoling how utterly they keep to one another for warmth and security.

LOVLINESS NEEDS NOT THE AID
OF FOREIGN ORNAMENT, BUT IS,
WHEN UNADORNED, ADORNED
THE MOST.

— JAMES THOMPSON

(1700 – 1748)

It was a wonderful day for the sanctuary when beautiful Honey arrived. It was a fortunate day for Honey too, since she had suffered terribly. Honey had been hit by a car as a starving mother out looking for food. Somewhere she had a litter of puppies. No one knew where. Honey's right front leg had been irreparably injured, requiring amputation; she had lost a leg and her puppies all in one afternoon. Probably Honey had been abandoned. She was thin and weak and her coat was sparse and short. Over time this angelic dog has become ravishingly beautiful. Love is her way of life. Her brown eyes are deep and sparkling with a reverence for life.

To love and to be loved —

this on earth

is the highest bliss.

— Heinrich Heine

(1797 - 1856)

Out under the vast skies my love for the rescued dogs comes home. Nature seems to have implanted so much love and gratitude in these humble living creatures. They seem so grateful just to have someone to go for a walk with them every day, and I am so grateful to take the walk with them. Each one, more precious by far than gold, is a true friend for life.

HUNGERING, HUNGERING,
HUNGERING, FOR PRIMAL
ENERGIES AND NATURE'S
DAUNTLESSNESS.

— WALT WHITMAN

(1819 – 1892)

The two young beauties were rescued from deprivation, from a cruel land. Though starved and ill, the freedom and health of sanctuary life brought them great happiness. These two siblings, females, are Irish wolfhound crosses, named Emmie and Fudge. The two are deeply bonded and together they will stay. Their enthusiasm for life is like a swelling of waves each day. Emmie and Fudge play complicated games of hide, sneak, and chase in the forest, perhaps an ancestral influence from their wolf heritage. They kindle energy in all of us, yet they rest like sleepy angels through the night. Their rest is a salve in preparation for the exciting horizons of tomorrow.

THIS IS JUST THE WAY
WITH SOME PEOPLE...
THEY GET DOWN ON A THING
WHEN THEY DON'T KNOW
NOTHING ABOUT IT.

— MARK TWAIN

(1834 - 1910)

Our very precious Dachsund mix mother dog, Alice, was rescued out from under a wood pile in Northern
New Mexico with her four newborn puppies. Piper, who looks most, and behaves most like his devoted mother,
burrows into any and all holes, depressions, and cavities. His hopes of coming up and out with a treasure, dead or alive, is unbounded.

IF, INSTEAD OF A GEM,
OR EVEN A FLOWER,
WE COULD CAST THE GIFT
OF A LOVELY THOUGHT INTO
THE HEART OF A FRIEND,
THAT WOULD BE GIVING AS
THE ANGELS GIVE.

— GEORGE MacDONALD

(1824 - 1905)

Among the most peaceful animals at the sanctuary are the rabbits. Every pose appears meditative or contemplative.
They have arrived here for various reasons … not wanted anymore, a broken leg, life was too busy for a rabbit … It is a great
pleasure to go about the business of feeding the rabbits, and they look so utterly grateful as they become contentedly immersed
in colorful piles of lettuce, parsley, carrots, grapes, strawberries, and don't forget the white millet and Quaker oats.
The rabbits nibble at each other too, and lean against each other in loving repose.

WHATEVER YOU ARE BY NATURE,
KEEP TO IT;   NEVER DESERT
YOUR OWN LINE OF TALENT.
BE WHAT NATURE INTENDED YOU FOR,
AND YOU WILL SUCCEED;
BE ANYTHING ELSE AND YOU WILL
BE TEN THOUSAND TIMES WORSE
THAN NOTHING.

— SYDNEY SMITH

(1771 - 1845)

It is fascinating to perceive that each puppy in a litter was born as an individual character.
Even though a litter of seven pups is black with white toes, or another litter is all yellow with tan ears, each pup
is special with its own perceptions and psychology. Each one is distinguishable from the group in some special way.
A born leader, for example, will exhibit marked individuality and quality within five weeks of life.

NEVER HOLD ANYONE BY THE
BUTTON, OR THE HAND,
IN ORDER TO BE HEARD OUT;
FOR IF PEOPLE ARE UNWILLING
TO HEAR YOU, YOU HAD BETTER
HOLD YOUR TONGUE THAN THEM.

— PHILLIP D.S. CHESTERFIELD
(1694 – 1773)

The rescued dogs of the sanctuary vary in size, age, and temperament. These differences bring on playfulness, trickery and wit. Dogs of varying size and age enjoy games of pretending and subjugation. They come to know one another well, to trust, and to invite the game again and again. Diversions and amusements are a natural and healthy part of every day.

TO CALL HIM A DOG HARDLY
SEEMS TO DO HIM JUSTICE;
THOUGH INASMUCH AS HE HAD
FOUR LEGS, A TAIL, AND
BARKED, I ADMIT HE WAS,
TO ALL OUTWARD APPEARANCES.
BUT TO THOSE OF US WHO
KNEW HIM WELL, HE WAS A
PERFECT GENTLEMAN.

— HERMOINE GINGOLD

(1897 - 1987)

Spirit, Heart and Soul Animal Sanctuary top dog, was found at a gas station as a starving puppy. Who could have known what an extraordinary dog this pup would grow up to be? He protects all animals coming into the sanctuary. He greets visitors at the gate and escorts them down the driveway. Spirit keeps all coyotes at bay in his mountainous forest home. At just one yip of the coyote he is into the forest with his charges following suit. He understands the protocol. He comprehends order, responsibility, gentleness, and challenge. And yes, Spirit is his mistress's best pal and comrade, for life.

ONE CAN SAVOR SIGHTS AND SOUNDS
MORE DEEPLY WHEN ONE GETS REALLY
OLD.
IT MAY BE THE LAST TIME YOU SEE
A SUNSET, A TREE, THE SNOW, OR
KNOW SUMMER.
THE SEA, A LAKE, ALL BECOME AS
IN CHILDHOOD, A GREAT WONDER:
THEN SEEN FOR THE FIRST TIME,
NOW PERHAPS FOR THE LAST.
MUSIC, BIRD SONG, THE WIND,
THE WAVES ———
"LOVING WELL", TO BORROW FROM
SHAKESPEARE'S 73RD SONNET,
" THAT WHICH I MUST LEAVE
ERE LONG."

——— HELEN NEARING

(1904 - 1995)

Traveling through the Hopi reservation I found some dogs in need.
I took three home with me. One, a black lab, was especially mournful and shy.
She had never been in a house before. She sat in the parking lot, watching me.
I talked with her; the gentle soul made my heart ache. It was hard,
but she slowly followed my meager crock of butter into my room.
We ate together, spent the night in simplicity, she became mine,
and I became hers. For ten beautiful years our hearts shared life and love.

HOME, THE SPOT OF EARTH

SUPREMELY BLEST,

A DEARER, SWEETER SPOT

THAN ALL THE REST.

~ ROBERT MONTGOMERY

(1807 - 1855)

Over the hills and valleys of life the horses pass. Some especially sensitive and beautiful ones have lived their lives out in peace
at the sanctuary. Their home is their heaven. Precious, sixteen years into life, was wounded as a polo pony.
Now she lives without demands, living each day at her own tranquil and undisturbed pace.

IF YOU HAVE MEN WHO WILL
EXCLUDE ANY OF GOD'S CREATURES
FROM THE SHELTER OF COMPASSION
AND PITY, YOU WILL HAVE
MEN WHO WILL DEAL LIKEWISE
WITH THEIR FELLOW MEN.

— ST. FRANCIS OF ASSISI

(1181 — 1226)

At the age of one month, Emmie came to the sanctuary along with her sister.
The puppies had been found in a desolate area of the Southwest; they were thin, weak, malnourished and ill.
Yet the pups, Emmie and Fudgie, conveyed a passion for life and they became inextricably wound around my heart.

THE MOST BEAUTIFUL THINGS

IN THE WORLD CANNOT BE

SEEN OR EVEN TOUCHED.

THEY MUST BE FELT BY

THE HEART.

— HELEN KELLER

(1880 — 1968)

Little Nana came to the sanctuary as an abandoned mother. She had four tiny puppies with her. Three were weak and very premature. They died. The fourth is robust and lively, becoming a delightful part of the world. Nana is now happy and loved. Her dream came true.

LOVE IS PATIENT AND KIND;
LOVE IS NOT JEALOUS OR BOASTFUL;
IT IS NOT ARROGANT OR RUDE.
LOVE DOES NOT INSIST ON ITS OWN WAY;
IT IS NOT IRRITABLE OR RESENTFUL;
IT DOES NOT REJOICE AT WRONG,
BUT REJOICES IN THE RIGHT.
LOVE BEARS ALL THINGS,
BELIEVES ALL THINGS,
HOPES ALL THINGS.

— PAUL

(A.D.   1ST CENTURY)

Many beautiful horses have been rescued by the sanctuary. They are granted lives of tranquility and plenty. No demands are placed on our rescued horses. Most have been abused and hungry before. There is always another horse there for each one to bond with, to love. Love between horses is profound, which permits the full unfolding of their personal peace.

THE GREATEST THOUGHTS ARE
GRASPED LAST...
THE LIGHT OF THE MOST DISTANT
STAR REACHES MAN LAST,
AND BEFORE IT HAS ARRIVED,
EVERY PERSON DENIES THAT THERE
IS SUCH A STAR.

— FRIEDRICH NIETZCHE

(1844 - 1900)

This lovely male puppy has a star-light quality, so beautiful a creation that it is hard to take one's eyes away. This puppy was found lost and abandoned in a remote area of Arizona and was delivered with others to the sanctuary. Such puppies have suffered fear, insecurity, and starvation. Their eyes can tell the tale. But they have set their sail to survive, and have earned a special grace.

DEAR GOD,

BE GOOD TO ME →

THE SEA IS SO WIDE

AND MY BOAT IS SO SMALL.

— A BRETON FISHERMAN'S PRAYER

This handsome puppy arrived at the sanctuary knowing nothing of good humans, only scary ones. Fortunately she was only four weeks old and was able to recover from this first impression. She was adopted into a wonderful home with a male pup of similar age. At the sanctuary we attend carefully to fearful puppies, spending many gentle and compassionate hours. Many a terrified abused pup has learned to trust and life can be lived joyously.

IT SHOULD NOT BE BELIEVED
THAT ALL BEINGS EXIST FOR
THE SAKE OF MAN.
ON THE CONTRARY, ALL THE OTHER
BEINGS TOO HAVE BEEN INTENDED
FOR THEIR OWN SAKES AND NOT
FOR THE SAKE OF SOMETHING ELSE.

— MOSES MAIMONIDES

(A.D. 1135 - 1204)

On the edge of Spirit Canyon, once an ancient sea bed 350 million years ago, the rescued dogs hunt and play like their ancestors of the wild. Rabbits, chipmunks and squirrels give reason for chase. The wildness of the place itself inspires a dog to go back to his true nature, at peace with the idea of the hunt. There is merriment and bravery in their wildness, another home they understand.

THE ONE ABSOLUTELY UNSELFISH
FRIEND THAT MAN CAN HAVE IN
THIS SELFISH WORLD, THE ONE
THAT NEVER DESERTS HIM,
THE ONE THAT NEVER PROVES
UNGRATEFUL OR TREACHEROUS,
IS HIS DOG ...
WHEN ALL OTHER FRIENDS
DESERT, HE REMAINS.

— SENATOR GEORGE GRAHAM VEST

IN 1884

There is indeed an inexplicable bond between dog and man. I can go on walks every day with some of the same sanctuary dogs, for years.
They never tire of my company, nor I of theirs. There is always something more to sense, to feel, to discuss, to see, to do.
We go together, walk together, play together, watch the birds together, and go home together.
Every evening is one of peace and love since we remain happily, devotedly, together.

Sometimes it seems that people hear best what we do not say.

— Eric Hoffer
(1902 - 1983)

Thoughtful and observant Posie has lived for many years at the sanctuary. She was rescued from abandonment at one year of age. Posie is admirably contained and quiet unless visitors and old friends arrive. Then she wiggles and barks with great joy. Posie seems to possess wisdom. Her quiet way of life is her choice for it provides peace. Posie tells us that the deepest rivers flow with the least sound.

PEACE IS THE EVENING STAR
OF THE SOUL, AS VIRTUE
IS ITS SUN; AND THE TWO
ARE NEVER FAR APART.

— CALEB C. COLTON

(1780 - 1832)

Animals find peace and happiness as they look out into the evening air.
The sun's bright light has faded and twilight brings a welcome calm and coolness into the mountains.
The ravens have just departed, calling prayer-like messages to one another. All the animals are at rest in preparation for another joyful day.

THE WORLD IS SUCH A BUSY PLACE,

THERE'S SO MUCH HURRY IN IT.

ISN'T IT SO NICE SOMETIMES

TO PAUSE FOR JUST A MINUTE . . .

— UNKNOWN

These busy days, dogs seem to have a far easier time pausing than humans do. The dogs pause and rest many times during their happy, playful, busy days. It is most enjoyable to feel their calm. Both these little dogs, Timmy and Dreamy, who are now good friends, came from the same large city pound euthanasia lists. Many small dogs are found abandoned and are consequently in very poor physical condition to say nothing of exhausted and frightened. Both Timmy and Dreamy are saintly creatures; they are, happily, permanent sanctuary residents.

LITTLE THINGS CAN OFTEN

BE

THE BIGGEST THINGS IN

SOMEONE'S DAY.

→ UNKNOWN

The animals are entertained and fulfilled by what humans call little things. But there is such joy and beauty in the "little things"; perhaps they are not so little. Little things come with great consequences. A tiny puppy lost ... is that a little thing? The tiny puppy becomes someone's best love and two lives are blessed—a big thing. Every creature's comfort is secured by a little more charity, a little more devotion, a little more fun, a little warm bed; just ask the rescued dogs.

EVERY NOW AND AGAIN
TAKE A GOOD LOOK AT SOMETHING
NOT MADE WITH HANDS —
A MOUNTAIN, A STAR, THE TURN
OF A STREAM.
THERE WILL COME TO YOU
WISDOM AND PATIENCE AND SOLACE
AND, ABOVE ALL, THE ASSURANCE
THAT YOU ARE NOT ALONE IN THE WORLD.

— SIDNEY LOVETT

Given the opportunity, dogs and other animals are thoroughly involved with the natural world. They will contentedly go home with their human friend and sleep on a woven bed, but give a dog a hill to climb, a stream to run through, a valley to hunt in, a log to chew, a hole to dig, and their day is rich as gold. The dogs look into the distance, ears arise, eyes alert, paws a-ready, prepared to catch the slightest whiff on the breeze or movement on the ground. This is their real world; may they have their chance to enjoy it.

TWO MEN TROD THE WAY OF LIFE;
THE FIRST, WITH DOWN-CAST EYE;
THE SECOND, WITH AN EAGER FACE
UPLIFTED TO THE SKY.

HE WHO GAZED UPON THE GROUND SAID,
"LIFE IS DULL AND GRAY."
BUT HE WHO LOOKED INTO THE STARS
WENT SINGING ON HIS WAY.

— UNKNOWN

Dogs have many moods and feelings just as people do. Some dogs are born with a certain disposition, such as Spirit, our sanctuary top dog, who is a gentlemanly leader. Some are given to whim and caprice. Some seem to like to cuddle forever; some are much more watchful and observant than others; some are the center of the universe; others love the pack. Some dogs are much better guard dogs than others; some are talented hunters while others sit and watch the pursuit. However we perceive them, dogs are wonderful and lovable friends.

NO MATTER HOW RIGHTLY THE
BODY MAY BE CHAINED TO THE
WHEEL OF DAILY DUTIES,
THE SPIRIT IS FREE . . .
TO BEAR ITSELF AWAY FROM NOISE
AND VEXATION INTO THE SECRET
PLACES OF THE MOUNTAINS.

— UNKNOWN

There are so many secret places in the mountains that it is a joy each time the dogs find another one.
It would be easy to suddenly find oneself lost, so we have to mark our trail carefully. The dogs are spirited by new
finds, new caves and new bends. What a pleasure to share their elation, especially in the vast, eternal quiet of the mountains.

Someday I'll sail my little
boat

upon the finest sea

but all I really want is you,

for all eternity.

— Natalie Owings

The wistful black puppy was rescued with his siblings and his mother just in time. It was cold and coyotes were around.
They were brought safely to the sanctuary. I have never experienced such love as that which comes from dogs.
Even little puppies are prepared to spend the whole day, the whole week, their whole lives just with a person. There is a look of longing
when they wish to be held, and another look of yearning when they wish you to just sit with them and talk and watch the sun go down.

I HAVE WEPT IN THE NIGHT
FOR THE SHORTNESS OF SIGHT →
THAT TO SOMEBODY'S NEED
I WAS BLIND ;
BUT I NEVER HAVE YET
FELT A TINGE OF REGRET
FOR BEING A LITTLE TOO KIND .

→ UNKOWN

So many times a person has been concerned that they might treat a dog or puppy too well … he or she might become "spoiled."
But dogs and puppies respond to love and good times and good food with a wealth of respect and sheer happiness.
Dogs love to love and they understand what love is whether it is coming to them or going from them. Good times and nice
soft beds and delicious food are manifestations of the love you have for your dog. Spoiling is a human issue; just love your dog all you can.

THE GREATEST HAPPINESS OF LIFE
IS THE CONVICTION THAT WE ARE LOVED,
LOVED FOR OURSELVES, OR RATHER
LOVED IN SPITE OF OURSELVES.
LIFE IS A FLOWER, OF WHICH
LOVE IS THE HONEY.

— VICTOR HUGO

(1802 - 1885)

Love is bountiful among puppies. Although they have scraps, egos and jealousies, puppies look to one another for love and support.
This is a law of nature in puppies. The sanctuary litters of rescued puppies are so full of love as to be bursting.
As time goes on the puppy sits at his master's feet asking for love, speaking of love in his eyes.
The life of a puppy turns into a quest for love. The life of a dog is all about love, given freely and profusely to some fortunate soul.

SPRING! SO THEN THE YEAR
IS REPEATING ITS OLD STORY AGAIN.

WE ARE COME ONCE MORE TO ITS
MOST CHARMING CHAPTER.
THE VIOLETS AND THE MAY
FLOWERS ARE AS ITS INSCRIPTIONS
OR VIGNETTES.
IT ALWAYS MAKES A PLEASANT
IMPRESSION UPON US,
WHEN WE OPEN AGAIN AT
THESE PAGES OF THE BOOK OF LIFE.

— JOHANN WOLFGANG GOETHE

(1749 - 1832)

Such a joyous and delicate production, whatever the time of year, is a litter of newborn puppies. At the sanctuary they are always rescued puppies, sometimes with, sometimes without, their mothers. If they are found in winter they must stay indoors for warmth; if found in spring or summer, they will be frolicking in the warm sun as early as two and a half weeks of age. For any visitor, young or old, little puppies strike notes of the precious and joyous wrapped into one. Another page of the book of life is opened.

LIKE A MORNING DREAM,
LIFE BECOMES MORE AND MORE
BRIGHT THE LONGER WE LIVE,
AND THE REASON FOR EVERYTHING
APPEARS MORE CLEAR.
WHAT HAS PUZZLED US BEFORE
SEEMS LESS MYSTERIOUS,
AND THE CROOKED PATHS LOOK
STRAIGHTER AS WE APPROACH
THE END.

— JEAN PAUL RICHTER

(1768 - 1826)

Stacia was a small dog in stature but she proved to have a heart as big as all the world. We saved Stacia at the age of eleven from euthanasia. After living all those years, someone took Stacia to an animal shelter to end her life. But it was meant to be that Stacia came to the sanctuary to live her last three immensely happy years. She had her teeth cleaned, a hernia resolved, two cancerous tumors removed, and she started on medicine for an enlarged heart. Stacia blossomed, smiled, came on long walks with us, and was loved by all the dogs and by every human being she met. We all wish to be beside Stacia for all eternity.

EACH SPECIES IS A MASTERPIECE,

A CREATION ASSEMBLED WITH

EXTREME CARE AND GENIUS.

— EDWARD O. WILSON

(1929 -

Little Piper was born under a wood pile in northern New Mexico. His mother, Alice, was abandoned as a pregnant dog.
The family was rescued when the puppies were two days old, and brought to the sanctuary.
They all flourished and grew, becoming beautiful and very sought after for adoption.
Little Piper lives permanently at the sanctuary with his devoted mother. From cold and abandonment into warmth and love.

A GOOD MAN AND A WISE MAN
MAY AT TIMES BE ANGRY
WITH THE WORLD, AT TIMES
GRIEVED FOR IT;
BUT TO BE SURE, NO MAN WAS EVER
DISCONTENTED WITH THE WORLD
WHO DID HIS DUTY IN IT.

— ROBERT SOUTHEY

(1774 - 1843)

Spirit, the Heart and Soul Animal Sanctuary top dog, impresses visitors with his great size and gentleness.
What is deeper down in Spirit is his desire to fulfill his profound sense of duty.
Spirit appears to consider duty the grandest of ideas, and, as George Eliot wrote, the reward of one duty done is the power to fulfill another.
Spirit is primarily an Austrian shorthair Pinscher. How such a fine breed of dog could be found as a stray puppy at a gas station is a mystery.
He is powerful for his size and bravely guards his territory, the sanctuary, and is loyal beyond description to his owner, his best friend.
It is an honor to live with such a guard, and with a creature who knows that life's daily duties and daily bread are the sweetest things of life.

ONE OF THE FIRST CONDITIONS

OF HAPPINESS IS THAT THE

LINK BETWEEN MAN AND NATURE

SHALL NOT BE BROKEN.

— Leo Tolstoy

(1829 - 1910)

Nature makes herself known to be in charge of the mountains. All of us beings living in the mountains, regardless of species, regard nature with awe and respect. The sheer power of her wind and rain rightly frightens the dogs. The breadth of her mountains, the crash of her lightning and depth of snow, the sheer vastness of her sky seem to be her signatures of the ages. But then, in spring, a certain lazy joy enraptures the animals and they all reflect her warmth and the sparkle of her sun through the trees. Everyone is relaxed again. Soft breezes wrap like garlands throughout the sanctuary. The mountains are aglow again; the forest provides her shade, and every puppy is finding life exquisite in her unruffled calm.

THE BEST KIND OF FRIEND
IS THE FRIEND YOU CAN SIT
ON A PORCH WITH,
NEVER SAY A WORD,
AND THEN WALK AWAY
LIKE IT WAS THE BEST
CONVERSATION EVER.

— UNKNOWN

Wandering through the forest with all the dogs is indeed akin to having a long conversation with nature. Nature is always right there, all around, sometimes silent but often talkative with singing birds, yipping coyotes, the wind through the trees, barking dogs, or meandering, dripping water. Nature is always true and right. The dogs love nature as do all animals; nature is their favorite teacher. She unfolds countless secrets to them. Their hearts are thrilled and their minds calm. Nature is our daily friend and guide.

FRIENDSHIP IS THE SHADOW
OF THE EVENING ,
WHICH STRENGTHENS WITH
THE SETTING SUN
OF LIFE .

— JEAN DE LA FONTAINE

(1621 - 1695)

These dogs are the best of friends. Daisy, Missy, and Moosie are all less than a year old in this photograph.
All three were found abandoned in different places as little puppies at less than six weeks old.
Today, watching these beautiful young dogs play together is a perfect reminder of how fulfilling it is to rescue
abandoned puppies. Daisy, Missy and Moosie would all have touching stories to tell about their difficult beginnings.
But they are free of hardship now, free to express and live in sheer happiness every day. Their friendship is the sunshine of their lives.

MOST MARVELOUS AND ENVIABLE
IS THAT FECUNDITY OF FANCY
WHICH CAN ADORN WHATEVER IT
TOUCHES, WHICH CAN INVEST
DRY REASONING WITH UN-LOOKED
FOR BEAUTY,
MAKE FLOWERS BLOOM ON THE BROW
OF A PRECIPICE, AND EVEN
TURN THE ROCK ITSELF INTO
MOSS AND LICHENS.

— THOMAS FULLER

(1608 - 1661)

Rabbits and beautiful chickens are thriving at the sanctuary. In one special case, a handsome rooster is hopelessly in love with a male rabbit whose name is My-Bunny. The two cavort, play games, and sit together as though philosophizing. My-Bunny plays leap frog with his rooster; first he nibbles on rooster's feathers, followed by a nimble leap over his rooster's back. Rooster stands still for this, at full attention. Then My-Bunny nibbles again at rooster's feathers, and leaps back over to the first side. They portray a sensitive, respecting, and mutual adoration relationship.

ONE KERNEL IS FELT IN A
HAYSHED;
ONE DROP OF WATER HELPS TO
SWELL THE OCEAN;
A SPARK OF FIRE HELPS TO
GIVE LIGHT TO THE WORLD.
NONE ARE TO SMALL, TOO FEEBLE
TOO POOR TO BE OF SERVICE.
THINK OF THIS AND ACT.
LIFE IS NO TRIFLE.

— HANNAH MORE

(1745 - 1833)

Sarah, a beautiful golden retriever mix, lives her life at the sanctuary in many important roles, yet she is steadfastly Sarah.
Sarah was rescued from under a trailer in the middle of winter, surrounded by heavy snow, with ten newborn puppies.
No one was feeding her; she was emaciated. Two of her puppies had already died. We dug Sarah and her pups out from under
the trailer and brought them safely to the warmth of the sanctuary. Sarah has blossomed into a queenly presence, very devoted to
her role as top female dog. She is Spirit's (top dog) best friend. She goes with him everywhere. The wolf can be seen in Sarah's heritage.
The delicate grace in her stride and the serious sparkle in her eyes speak of a special history; she is highly respected by one and all.

NOTHING IS RICH BUT THE
INEXHAUSTIBLE WEALTH OF NATURE.
SHE SHOWS US ONLY SURFACES
BUT SHE IS A MILLION FATHOMS
DEEP.

— RALPH WALDO EMERSON

(1803 - 1882)

It was an astounding sight … a litter of two week old puppies was seen in a metal box in the back of a pickup truck on a very hot summer day. We heard the driver of the pickup was on his was to a river to dispose of the puppies. How much money would he take for the puppies? Twenty dollars would do. Twenty dollars saved seven little lives that day. Hurriedly we unpiled the almost expired litter, sprinkled their soft bodies with cool water, and rushed them back to the sanctuary for shade, a soft bed, and feeding. The seven little lives became the summer's joy, as we watched them grow and play amongst the pines.

KITES RISE AGAINST, NOT WITH
THE WIND.
— NO MAN EVER WORKED HIS
PASSAGE ANYWHERE IN A DEAD
CALM.

— JOHN NEAL

(1793 - 1876)

The face of this fascinating dog reveals, to the sensitive person, a time of past misfortune. She arrived at the sanctuary as a small puppy, only two and a half months old, from a reservation. I named her Missy for her very feminine demeanor. It was apparent that little Missy had already been abused, and very badly. What had happened? Missy did not want to be touched and cuddled by humans, as most puppies do. She is growing up at the sanctuary, is happy and frequently playful. She will lick my hands and face, but swiftly, with a sense of caution. Slowly, so slowly, we show her peace, quiet, affection, and make no demands. Missy will grow and will rise to certain occasions on her own terms, in her own way. She knows she is loved and respected … like a beautiful feather … afloat somewhere …

GOD FORBID THAT I SHOULD
GO TO ANY HEAVEN IN
WHICH THERE ARE NO HORSES.

— R. GRAHAM

Many horses in the United States at this time (summer 2008) have no place to go. Many are being taken across the border into Mexico for slaughter. The horses are badly treated in this process. Everything is contrary to what a horse wants and needs. When I heard there were two mares and their newborn foals about to be slaughtered I decided to turn their fate around and had them rescued and brought to the sanctuary. All four were unwell, but time, good food and equine veterinary care could bring them all back to health and happiness. They all rested and fed in peace. The baby horses followed their mamas about; springtime was as it should be for two mares and their foals.

I DO NOT WANT THE PEACE
WHICH PASSETH UNDERSTANDING.
I WANT THE UNDERSTANDING
WHICH BRINGETH PEACE.

— HELEN KELLER

(1880 - 1968)

The feeling of peace at the very center—this is the peace known by new mothers. It has always been true; century after century of life shows new mothers and their infants to be truly at peace. In the sanctuary nursery this young mother dog, Mia, finally felt at peace and cared for. She had been found sitting next to a dumpster, on a dirty cloth, with her three newborn baby puppies, two days old. Someone saw the thin mother there, destitute, and rushed her to the sanctuary. It was an honor and deep pleasure to provide a home for beautiful Mia. She was a perfect mother, always peaceful, in perfect attendance to her little ones.

EVERY YEAR OF MY LIFE
I GROW MORE CONVINCED THAT
IT IS WISEST AND BEST TO
FIX OUR ATTENTION ON THE
BEAUTIFUL AND THE GOOD, AND
DWELL AS LITTLE AS POSSIBLE
ON THE EVIL AND THE FALSE.

— RICHARD CECIL

(1748 - 1777)

Puppies are made of beauty and peace. Newborns seem the essence of innocence so much so I take pause every time they come our way … so delicate and fragile as to be one of the finest creations of nature.
This litter of four newborns was found in a junkyard in southern New Mexico at the age of one day, without their mother. My heart cries for the mother dog from whom they were probably taken. The newborns were rushed to our veterinary hospital, put on heated blankets, and bottle fed. At four days old the pups were at the sanctuary, snuggled into a nursery with soft stuffed animals around them. The stuffed animals help to feel like mama. All four survived and grew into exquisitely beautiful dogs.

WHEN I WAS YOUNG I WAS
SURE OF EVERYTHING;
IN A FEW YEARS, HAVING BEEN
MISTAKEN A THOUSAND TIMES,
I WAS NOT HALF SO SURE OF
MOST THINGS;
AT PRESENT, I AM HARDLY
SURE OF ANYTHING BUT WHAT
LIFE HAS REVEALED TO ME.

— JOHN WESLEY

(1703 - 1791)

Many beautiful, youthful dogs have scampered and capered their way into adulthood at the sanctuary.
Both Moosie and Daisy, playing mock attack games together, possess an air of invincibility, so prevalent in the young of many species. It is interesting and amusing to observe the older and wiser dogs, as they ignore the "unconquerable" youngsters at their play.
Yet if the insuperable youngsters dare to trod presumptuously close to an elder, the older and wiser shall, with a deep and grave growl, catapult the young dogs back into their lowly positions.

THERE IS NOTHING SO GREAT
THAT I FEAR TO DO IT FOR
MY FRIEND; NOTHING SO SMALL
THAT I WILL DISDAIN TO DO
IT FOR HIM.

— SIR PHILIP SIDNEY

(1554 - 1586)

Our best friends are the most wonderful experiences in life. There is so much understanding, so much arm in arm. Yet friendships are fragile and must be honored and handled with care. Even during the harder days our friend is still a source of refuge and calm. And on the sunny days our friend is running by our side in joy. And in the evening our friend is as beautiful a gift as the golden, setting sun.

It is worth a thousand pounds a year to have the habit of looking on the bright side of things.

— Francis Johnson

(1562 - 1618)

It was on a cold day in March when the ground in these mountains was still damp from melting snow that a litter of four pups was found shivering at the sanctuary gate. These puppies were not in a box but simply left on the ground. Visitors to the sanctuary found them and carried the little trembling bodies in. We instantly prepared a nursery and warm formula. They engulfed the formula, so more and more was mixed. The smallest, Daffodil, above, could hardly stand up. But within 48 hours all the pups blossomed. Their small bodies were dirty and sticky … who cares! These were some of the most beautiful puppies to ever arrive.

TWO BEINGS CANNOT LONG
BE FRIENDS IF THEY CANNOT
FORGIVE EACH OTHER'S LITTLE
FAILINGS.

— JEAN DE LA BRUYÈRE

(1645 - 1696)

Dogs and puppies, amongst many other species, become profoundly good friends. They share their time, their beds, their food; they share experiences together, happiness, and most admirable of all is their capacity for forgiveness. Perhaps dogs are more brave and refined than us humans. Forgiveness saves the cost of anger and brings the mind to contentment. The dog always seeks easy reconciliation and never an opportunity to take revenge. The dog owes it to himself to remember events, and remember he does. But the sun will never set on anger.

UNTIL WE STOP HARMING
OTHER LIVING BEINGS,
WE ARE STILL SAVAGES.

— THOMAS A. EDISON

(1847 - 1931)

This lovely and intelligent two month old puppy was indeed rescued from "nowhere." He was found with his three siblings in a junkyard in southern New Mexico. This is bad enough; the puppies were only one day old. The tiny litter was rushed to our veterinary hospital where they were kept warm on heated bedding and syringe fed for several days. Puppies need nothing more than a warm, nursing mother, but amazingly all four survived. All four grew to be very beautiful dogs and all are adopted into loving homes in Colorado.

It is not a guiding spirit
that reveals to me secretly
in a flash what I must say
or do, but thought and
reflection.

— Napoleon

(1769 – 1821)

Spirit is the top dog at the Heart and Soul Animal Sanctuary. He grew to hold this position not only through his size but also through his most unusual character. Spirit was found as a starving three month old puppy at a gas station. Even in that setting he impressed the someone who rescued him, and who brought him to the sanctuary. Spirit has wisdom at his core. He understands his role as a gentle leader of all the other dogs. He has a policy of kindness, yet he is not faint of heart. If the sanctuary requires protection against intruders or coyotes or stray, unknown dogs, Spirit is out in front. The other dogs never doubt him. If there is a problem they know that Spirit knows. He accompanies the equine vet to help out the horses. He accompanies puppies to have their vaccinations. He escorts the visitors from the gate to the giant dog house. His self confidence is not offensive but, rather, admirable. He provides the sanctuary with strength and direction. Spirit is a truly great dog who found his calling.

THE GIFT OF LEARNING TO MEDITATE
IS THE GREATEST GIFT YOU CAN GIVE
YOURSELF IN THIS LIFE. FOR IT IS ONLY
THROUGH MEDITATION THAT YOU CAN
UNDERTAKE THE JOURNEY TO DISCOVER YOUR
TRUE NATURE, AND SO FIND THE STABILITY
AND CONFIDENCE YOU WILL NEED TO LIVE,
AND DIE, WELL.
MEDITATION IS THE ROAD TO ENLIGHTENMENT.

— SOGYAL RINPOCHE

When a dog is permitted plenty of time outdoors, in the natural world, one sees the dog contemplate. Dogs adore to gaze into the wilderness, to sit and watch and to feel of the natural environment around them. All the external forces of nature are as interesting to dogs as to us, maybe more so. They enjoy pondering and meditating, even studying the world around them. And so it is with our basset hound, Auntie May. She is thoroughly enjoying her peaceful contemplation of the forest covered mountains around her.

POVERTY OFTEN DEPRIVES A MAN
OF ALL SPIRIT AND VIRTUE;
IT IS HARD FOR AN EMPTY
BAG TO STAND UPRIGHT.

— BENJAMIN FRANKLIN

(1706 - 1790)

A very thin, almost skeletal white horse came through our gate one day, led by a man who "had no further use for this horse." My heart was enveloped by the old, white mare. Jasmine was her name and she was here to stay. Jasmine was starving to death because she had no good teeth left. Her teeth were not able to chew up grass or hay, which she was unsuccessfully attempting to exist on. I served Jasmine a large bowl of special food for horses mixed with warm water so as to make the grains soft. She loved every soft mouthful, swallowing contentedly again and again. Her eyes twinkled. In a few days Jasmine's spirit flowered. She gained weight. She trotted, nickered and whinnied. Adorable Jasmine graces the sanctuary with her inner and outer beauty.

WHEN THE HEART GOES BEFORE,
LIKE A LAMP, AND ILLUMINES
THE PATHWAY, MANY THINGS ARE
MADE CLEAR THAT ELSE LIE
HIDDEN IN DARKNESS.

— Henry Wadsworth Longfellow

Such a lovable, charming lover of life is Daisy. She is the dog who would carry your lamp up the mountain for you, and down the other side. Then Daisy would hunt in the woods until she found you a meal. Daisy would dig a fine hole for you to sleep in, and cover you with boughs to keep you warm. And through the darkest night Daisy would watch and listen throughout the hours to keep you from harm's way. How could such an extraordinary dog evolve out of a lost, emaciated puppy? Daisy came to the sanctuary at the tender age of three weeks, abandoned and hungry. She is our Daisy, cherished, now and forever.

THE DIGNITY, THE GRANDEUR,
THE TENDERNESS, THE EVERLASTING
AND DIVINE SIGNIFICANCE OF
MOTHERHOOD.

— THOMAS DE WITT TALMAGE

(1832 - 1902)

Mothers and their babies have graced the Heart and Soul Animal Sanctuary often. Each one and each occasion speak of the essence of love. The baby or babies are cherished, guided lovingly, tenderly, through their first days. The mothers watch, clean, and nurse with sublime joy. No words have the strength to express the power and majesty of the mother's love. And as the youngsters grow and play, the mothers are always nearby in fond devotion, aware of the journey to come.

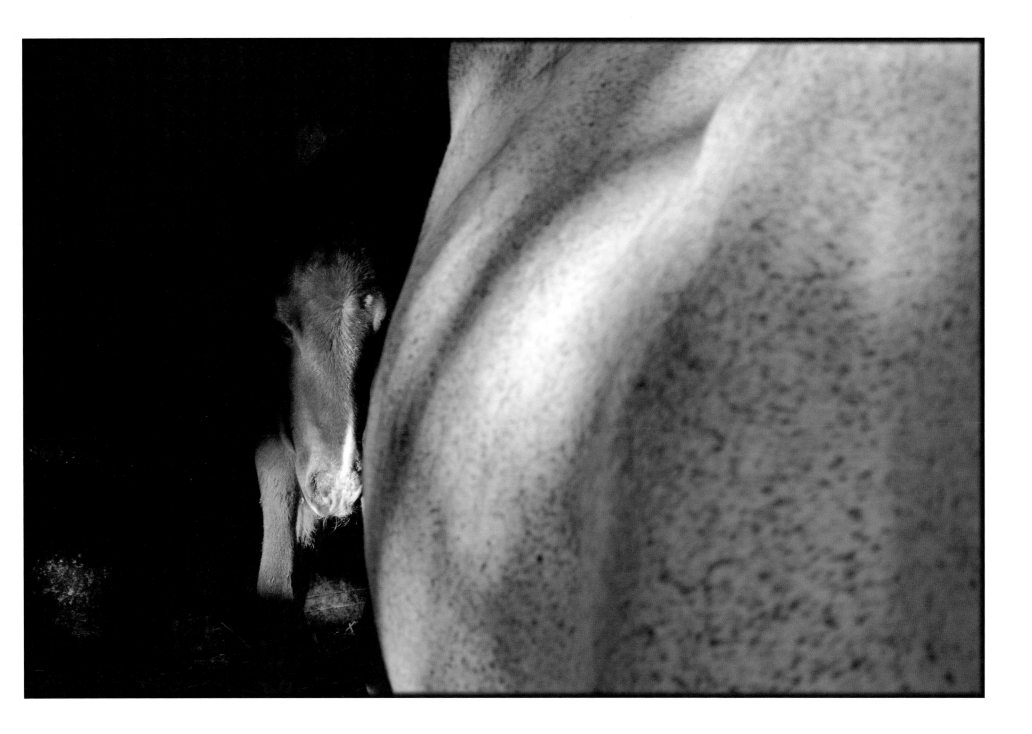

A MOTHER'S LOVE IS INDEED
THE GOLDEN LINK THAT BINDS
YOUTH TO AGE ;
AND HE IS STILL BUT A CHILD,
HOWEVER TIME MAY HAVE FURROWED
HIS CHEEK, OR SILVERED HIS BROW,
WHO CAN YET RECALL,
WITH A SOFTENED HEART,
THE FOND DEVOTION, OR THE GENTLE
CHIDINGS, OF THE BEST FRIEND
THAT GOD EVER GIVES US.

— CHRISTIAN NESTELL BOVEE

(1820 - 1904)

Reg, the larger, is the son of Gracie who attempts to reprimand, but simply adores her baby. It appears to be so with dogs, as it is with humans, that no matter how big or how old, the offspring is the eternal youngster in the mind of mother. All sanctuary mother dogs keep a baby. Much happiness is to be seen amongst these frolicking pairs. However, mother is always right; baby is always in the learning phase. Training and lessons at mother's knee are never forgotten; a breath of true life that clings onto the young heart for all the challenging years to come.

EVERY DAY IS A GIFT
I RECEIVE FROM HEAVEN ;
LET US ENJOY TODAY
THAT WHICH IT BESTOWS ON ME.
IT BELONGS NOT MORE TO
THE YOUNG MAN THAN TO ME,
AND TOMORROW BELONGS TO
NO ONE .

— MANCROIX

Peaches, Yuri and Perry … friends forever. Dogs have a wonderful ability to always be in a certain place, and not elsewhere. They are not inclined to bemoan the past and anticipate the future. They respond to the moment immediately without stumbling over stray thoughts. The dog will devote each day to the needs of that day, and hence the evening brings a welcome, unbothered rest. The dog can run in the field without busying himself with the events of tomorrow. He enjoys the blessings of his field, his day. Hopes and cares and apprehensions of disquietude are not the fiber of a dog's day; he will not wander through hours that are not there. Every day is the whole of life.

You will find that the
mere resolve not to be useless,
and the honest desire
to help others, will,
in the quickest and delicatest
ways, improve yourself.

— John Ruskin

(1819 – 1900)

The sanctuary is blessed and honored by the maternal presence of our wise basset hound, Auntie May. She is given to resolving difficulties and thus receives the insecure, wayward, motherless puppy willingly. The pups find warmth and security in being physically close to Auntie May; they will always seek her out. She seems to listen to them and permits them to crawl all over her. Most of the other grown dogs would tend to snap or growl at the migrating pups, but Auntie May has resolved to be of use and help. May the shy and wayward ones of the world come to find their Auntie May.

I HAVE SELDOM SEEN MUCH
OSTENTATION AND MUCH LEARNING
MET TOGETHER.
THE SUN, RISING AND DECLINING,
MAKES LONG SHADOWS;
AND MID-DAY, WHEN HE IS HIGHEST,
NONE AT ALL.

— BISHOP JOSEPH HALL

(1574 - 1656)

Is there a more pleasant sight in spring than a mare with her young foal?
The mare is so happy to have her long legged baby to nurture. The two are gentle with one another;
their ancestors through millions of years experienced this beautiful peace. Like all animals they have been the subject of
continual evolution, becoming larger and faster over time. Day by day the mare leads her foal around, teaching by showing. Their dignity
and refinement reflect an immense history including migrations and many lands. The sanctuary saved this mare and foal from slaughter.

GREAT IS HE WHO ENJOYS
HIS EARTHENWARE AS IF IT WERE
SILVER PLATE, AND NOT LESS
GREAT IS THE MAN TO WHOM
ALL HIS SILVER PLATE IS NO
MORE THAN EARTHENWARE.

— ROBERT LEIGHTON,
ARCHBISHOP

(1611 - 1684)

Many puppies have come to the sanctuary who have been malnourished and who feel hungry. They all tend to gobble up their food as fast as possible, thinking someone else will get it if they don't. Even very small puppies, three weeks to one month old, will growl and behave aggressively if they have been starved. Nothing could feel so miserable for a puppy as being hungry. They are not able to feel happy in any way until plenty of food is available. This recently rescued pup finds the food dish a very comfortable and perfectly reasonable place to take a rest. It feels good, smells good, and tastes wonderful. Let puppies be puppies.

CONSCIENCE IS THE ROOT OF
ALL TRUE COURAGE;
IF A MAN WOULD BE BRAVE,
LET HIM OBEY HIS
CONSCIENCE .

— JAMES F. CLARKE

(1810 - 1888)

Peaches has lived all her life with her rescued mother at the sanctuary. She is most notable in her very quiet nature. Peaches' mother, Auntie May, was found under a vehicle with seven newborn puppies. She was brought to the sanctuary where she raised her puppies and flourished. Auntie May, a beautiful tri-colored basset hound is adorable, and much loved. Her female pup, Peaches, loves her mother, but remains quiet, if not a bit aloof. Peaches speaks to everyone of dignity and softness; her silence and reserve suggest an unknown which is fascinating.

THE BASIS OF ALL ANIMAL RIGHTS
SHOULD BE THE GOLDEN RULE:
WE SHOULD TREAT THEM AS WE
WOULD WISH THEM TO TREAT US,
WERE ANY OTHER SPECIES IN OUR
DOMINANT POSITION.

— CHRISTINE STEVENS

(1980 –

Animals and humans can engage in togetherness and have a wonderful time. No one is boss; we are simply there together enjoying the day, the walk, the special time together. There is a relationship of equality under the immense sky. We all came from the same kinds of beginnings way back then. We all exist together yet none of us is completed. No one is finished; we are all moving on toward an inescapable destiny. Even the horizon beckons us all to stay together as one.

CARING FOR ANOTHER LIFE
IS ONE OF THE MOST AWESOME
RESPONSIBILITIES THAT NATURE
HAS TO OFFER.
EMBRACING SUCH A CONTRACT
IS ONE OF THE GREAT JOYS
OF LIFE.

— CARLO DE VITO

Rescuing abandoned and abused animals presents the sanctuary with demanding requirements.
Since every animal arrives ill or injured, we require diagnosis, advice, therapy, surgery, and many medications.
The sanctuary has always sought the best medical care available. Our veterinarians are caring, highly capable and professional people.
Some conditions are complicated. The sanctuary has rescued a great many litters of puppies from remote areas, and continues to do so.
Some are not well and cannot thrive. Most are lively and treatable. All have survived on garbage, scraps, and contaminated water.
Some animals have mange, tape worms, gastrointestinal parasites, broken bones requiring x-rays and surgery.
Some arrive with coccidosis showing signs of dehydration and weight loss. All these and more are
treatable. All the animals seem to understand that they are finally being loved and cared for.

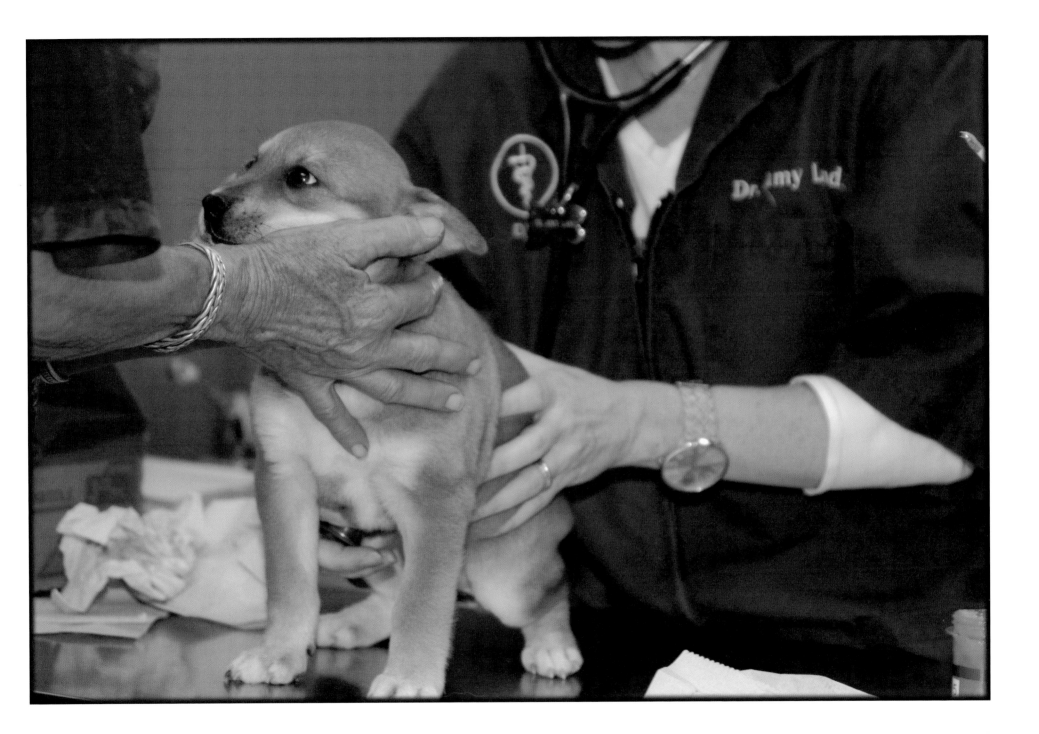

HAPPINESS IS LIKE A BUTTERFLY
WHICH, WHEN PURSUED, IS ALWAYS
BEYOND OUR GRASP,
BUT, IF YOU WILL SIT DOWN
QUIETLY, MAY ALIGHT UPON YOU.

— NATHANIEL HAWTHORNE

(1804 - 1864)

Puppies are intently inquisitive about one another. They test one another, which is also a test of where they stand in relation to each other. They make one another very happy and secure through play and companionship. But they can become quite feisty and self centered as well. Developing relationships and barriers in a group is an important precursor to life in the grown up world. At the sanctuary we do not permit any dog or pup to behave aggressively toward a younger, smaller puppy. Harmony and patience is encouraged.

DOES THE ROAD WIND UPHILL
ALL THE WAY?

YES, TO THE VERY END.

WILL THE JOURNEY TAKE THE
WHOLE LONG DAY?

FROM MORN TO NIGHT MY FRIEND.

— CHRISTINA ROSSETTI

Whatever must be done throughout the day, we must always include the journey.
The dogs, as many as thirty, find purpose and joy in running or meandering up and down, over and through the mountainous terrain.
The game of chase and hunting is always part of the journey; the youngsters are full of enthusiastic energy.
The old ones walk along absorbing the breeze, the view, the special time, from morn to night to journey's end.

The Heart & Soul ANIMAL SANCTUARY